The Way Magellan Must Have Felt

Poems by
Dwaine Spieker

Rogue Faculty Press

The author and publishers are grateful to the editors of the following publications, where some of these poems first appeared: *The Milford Free Press, The Nebraska Poets' Calendar, Nebraska Life, Plainsongs,* and *Midwest Quarterly.*

Copyright©2014 by Dwaine Spieker
ISBN: 978-0-692-22102-0
First Edition

Cover art by Calvin Banks
Author photo by Mollie Spieker

www.roguefacultypress.org

CONTENTS

For Mollie

∞

The near grows out of the far.

—Neihardt

Seagulls in Nebraska

They flock over this unplanted field
as if it were a Gulf

or Great Lake.
What matter hills and tides,

what matters latitude
high up, in open space?

Surfaces forever undulate. Heights
are always heights

and all flight is everywhere the same.

At One End of His Life

stood the Depression, the War,
and the Blizzard of '49.

He always spoke of them
then went silent a long time.

At the other end stood
the death of my grandmother.

He spoke of that for almost a year
then went silent forever.

Trees in April

The sharp shadows
                    of bare branches
have scraped the same
                    grim ground
every day since December.
                            Now at long last
frost is farther off,
                    branch-blades
blunt and rust,
                and dawns and days
promise more
                than the same swipes
with the same swords.
                            The winter-war
has calmed, is quiet,
                        and these fast fighters,
these hale heroes
                    and steady survivors,
weave war-tales
                    in tapestries of leaves
and gift the gold
                    torques and helmets
of spring sun
                to loyal warriors.

Town Park in Spring

The songs of robins sound like rusty swings,
back and forth all afternoon, here in April,
at the town park, where I've brought my kids
to play while I read the new *Sports Illustrated*.
Other birds play too—bluejays at tag,
cardinals at tetherball, a flock of sparrows
squeaking on an aural merry-go-round.
For birds are like children, playing whatever
and wherever they wish, that kind of play
guided only by whim and pure excitement,
and children are like birds, all chirp and chitter
and flutter and float, until that avian play
scatters from them like startled blackbirds
and the fun they knew is suddenly reduced
to reading *Sports Illustrated*. Nothing we can do
will stop it, save read and play, play and read,
back and forth all afternoon, the robinsong
swinging all around us, April's first warm day.

Headstones

The headstones here
resemble robins,

slow birds of stone,
wings folded in.

They perch at the tips
of the limbs of time,

their spring too large
for anyone to sense,

their songs too high
for living pitch.

Spring Snow

This snow has given us
a mid-growth hiatus,

a sweet, midwinter sleep
a month into spring.

By this time next week
we will bear the first heat,

be far gone on pilgrimage,
on that natural quest

toward blade, shoot, and leaf.
But for now let us savor

this respite from April,
a fast, an abstinence,

a mid-bud sabbatical.

After a Cold Front

April, and finally warm again,
so bright that even these dead
have come home early from work,
and here in our town's backyard,
facing west, they've lain back
in hammocks of new grass,
their hardbacks open to the wind.

Acoustic Guitarist

Dressed in black,
he takes requests
of classic rock.

For hours on end,
he sings every song
the crowd sends in.

But he knows more
lyrics and riffs
than he could perform

in any one night.
He knows the music
of traveling light.

Sunny and Windy

—town cemetery

Perfect weather, here in spring,
for flying kites, so today these dead
lift and loft the particolored
shapes of their souls, which dart and dive
and spin and rise in the high light
and warm wind, their headstones
anchoring the flight like spools of string.

Graduate

Today we'll all stand at attention
whenever you walk in, saluting you
as if your gown were a calm flag
to which we pledge our old allegiance.
Forgive us if today you stand as more
than your accomplishments, but as a banner
for each of us, our lives, our liberties,
and our pursuits of happiness. We salute
you, as well as the stars and stripes
of our own dreams, wild and actual,
and where we stand in them. Graduate,
you are our old glory made new again,
one nation under God, indivisible,
with liberty and justice for all.

May

— for Elna

Spring is up early this morning,
doing the laundry. In particular
she's hand-washing her sweaters,
soaking them all in cold dew

and draping their colorful wool
on trees around the neighborhood—
over lilacs, magnolias, and crabs,
over cherries and flowering pears.

A small job, an annual labor.
Soon enough all these blossoms
will evaporate like rinsewater;
soon enough all these garments

will be folded away and stored
deep in memory's antique dresser.
They're just too warm to be worn,
too plush to stay plush in summer.

At the Edge of Town

Late May, and warm, one of the first
deeply warm days, warm enough to go swimming,
and all the houses along this avenue
seem to have done just that, for, having emerged
up out of the hills, they now rest their elbows
on the poolside of the street. There,
lawn-to-lawn, conversing of bluebirds, perennials,
and young gardens, they float all afternoon,
slowly kicking their legs behind them
under the sparkling surface of the fields.

Sunrise, Early June

Someone has thrown the tennis ball
of the sun way over the horizon,
and the big black Labrador
of night has chased after it
and come huffing back, his breath
hot with running, the ball's surface
slick with drool, dropping it
right at the feet of daylight
to be thrown again, this time farther.

June

Now the birdsong has actually
retreated slightly.

Fewer are the declarations
of robins,

lessened are the calls
of cardinals.

Now birdsong is more indirect,
more peripheral,

more permanently woven
into the overall pattern.

Now song is part
of the way things are,

not simply
the way things ought to be.

Red-Headed Finch

The cardinal color of its head
fades to subtext
somewhere below the neck.

The nuance, the subtlety,
of the finch!
A sense of irony

that cardinals,
in their straightforwardness,
miss.

Rainbow Trout

If I conform,
it will be to my own spine,
the river of my sinews.

If I give in,
it will be to natural direction,
not current force.

If I obey,
it will be toward something far upstream,
the ancient faith.

Wren

Sometimes the present
wrens up in front of you,
distinct but nondescript.
You have to look for it.
When you were younger,
you thought each second
had to be a cardinal,
triumphant and red
in announcing itself.
But you'd have likely missed
this moment now, which
blends in with the bark,
no larger than a wren.
You had to look for it.

Garbage Truck

A thunderhead of metal,
a cumulonimbus cloud
in a sky of burnt diesel.

Today it hovers over
the streets of our town,
sucking up vapors,

updrafts of trash,
by hydraulic convection.
We hope it moves on.

Old Garage

It's hung around out back for years,
out near the alley, like a stray cat,
half-feral. Its peeling paint
stands up like fur, and the big door
caterwauls when you open it.
We don't do much to keep it here—
we only throw it scraps of wood,
a broken chair, and unused tools.
Yet often after roaming all night
it shows up again in the morning,
high on its haunches, proud of itself,
a dead mouse set before it as a gift.

Rain Gauge

He lives out in the suburbs now
in what used to be a cornfield,
yet still he keeps a gauge for rain
on his back fence. Although he grows
nothing anymore except his lawn,
although his office work goes on
oblivious to any season,
he can't forget the way a good, hard rain
shut tow-lines off for several days
and made his father's farm too wet
to fix fence or put up hay.
And so this morning, first thing,
before his long commute into the city,
he checks his gauge. An inch and a half
fell overnight, which still means rest,
a day off for the boy he used to be.

House

Ever so gently this morning,
it seems to rock back and forth
or side to side, a little boat
on a lake of rain. In it is my
tiny life, so small I don't need
far-off stars to help me navigate
the open, dark sea. My motion is
back-and-forth, side-to-side,
here and here again, home,
same house and same good life.

Sky

The fields stretch over the hills
as if the hills were not there.

The towns whorl outward
as if the fields were not there.

And in the towns the people
live and move, often unaware

of hills or fields or towns
or other people.

But the sky—wherever it is,
the sky cares.

Summer Constellations

Rare, frail
hidden flowers
over this
tropical weather.

Orchids.

A Herd of Cattle

—for Adam

Mid-morning, and the kind sunlight
sparkles over the great green waves
of the sandhills, through which these cattle
roll like dolphins, those lumbering
yet nimble swimmers of the open sea.

If life throws you overboard,
you can place trust in calm herds
of gentle creatures, cattle or dolphins,
to buoy you up and float you on
through kind light to warm shores.

Catch and Release

—for my sons

Before you begin, commit
to letting go every fish,
no matter the size,
no matter the kind.

Before you start, break
that cycle we have:
keeping the caught,
killing the kept,

eating the kill.
Before you even cast, say
you've hit your limit.
Then fish your fill.

A Grove of Cottonwoods

Although no doubt shipmasts were made
of harder timber, these cottonwoods
bear sails of leaves this afternoon,

and here you stand, plumb amidships,
on the oblong deck of this small grove
in tropical heat. A good trade wind

out of the south, you feel the ground
go wave-like underneath your legs,
certain but in a rolling pattern,

a constant motion. Here is your sea,
your frigate full of breath and being,
borne across the globe by leaves.

Radio Tower Lights

Hundreds of feet
above the horizon,

they blink red,
slow, kindhearted.

As warning signals,
they seem gentle,

graceful, confident.
I wish for that,

their brand of stern
but easy light.

I wish for that,
their calm, their height.

To a Friend

Tonight, at the blind
intersection of the present
and the distant past,
you ran that stop sign again.

You were speeding home.

Town Cemetery

Today its central lane
seems a long floating dock,

old cedars and pines
splashing up at the sides,

headstones bobbing like buoys.
So it takes a good moment

to regain your sea-legs,
step out, and begin to walk.

It's so hard to find balance
when your firmest footing

actually floats, floats atop
the waters of life and time,

but it helps to walk here often,
maintaining equilibrium,

your eyes on the distance,
on seagulls and ships.

Camel, County Fair

A local collector of exotic animals
has hauled this camel here today,
across the county, to be the main
attraction at the petting zoo.
But actually it's come so much
farther than that, through deserts,
over continents, seas, and oceans,
across millennia. For petting a camel
is nothing less than laying your hands
on the distant past, and feeling like
a nomad, a wanderer from somewhere
beyond the dunes of time, paused
at this colorful oasis of late summer,
the county fair, for rest and drink.
You too have come from far away,
the Fertile Crescent of your life,
to this sand-hot Saturday afternoon
in late July. And this dromedary,
you can tell, is feeling like
a beast of burden, already weary
of being such a center of attention.
Perhaps sensing a fellow traveler,
it lowers its long neck to look
right in your face: Where next?

Grain Elevator

Looking east,
arm raised,

a gray-green
statue of metal,

bearing a torch
of noonday sun

for the tired, the poor.

First Crickets

Now that their songs
nightly surround us,

we are able to say so much
and stay honest.

The world is deeper, more true
than we ever thought it,

more music than we knew
everywhere around us.

Crickets

The world is full of little songs.
They all reach your ears as you walk,
and some of them reach the treetops,
and some of those reach the stars.

By Myself in the Backyard

A lone cicada saxophones
and a piano answers, the ivory
of a single cricket, a jazz duet
on one of the last warm evenings.

Everyone in this private club
is missing someone, but these insects'
alternating solos let us know
the smooth duets of being alone.

Sunday Afternoon

Ever the good student,
autumn has been sprawled across

the carpet of our town,
finishing its homework,

the essay of the sky.
Today it further clarifies

the thesis of sunlight
with a few final details

of breeze. As, pen to teeth,
it simplifies

the syntax of the trees.

Moon

The full moon
walks home

with a big paper
bag of groceries.

The dawn air,
as cool as a gallon

of milk, smells
of bread and celery.

Dead Pine Tree

The spider of Pine Wilt
has built this brown web
between two cedars.

Its design is almost
infinitely intricate,
the web attractive

to anything that lives,
anything with the clear
insect wings of care.

Friday Night

As I stand next to a chain-link fence
at the high-school football game,
I notice, down to my left,
a small spider deftly crossing
over the diamonds of wire
as if I were a plump, oblivious,
middle-aged dragonfly
caught up, helpless and hapless,
in the intricate metal web
of wishing I were young again.

Football

A perfect evening of falling leaves,
and I am out back with my children,
playing football, teaching them
the basic idea of passing routes.
I show each one a simple pattern—
the hook, post, and square-out—
settle in to play quarterback,
then hike the ball. All three kids
run their routes, run them textbook,
and there is even one split-second
when all three are looking back,
hands up, just as I showed them,
wide open with hope and happiness.

Just then I discover my error,
that there is no way to throw
to all three at once, my boys
and my girl, to complete this play
without choosing one—that is,
no way with a regular football
to throw all three one perfect spiral.

Southwest

Now the sun is no larger
than my wife's shoulder.

As she goes to bed
in the southwest, she pulls

a comforter of clouds
up to her neck, then rolls over

into her dreams. She shines
long, long afterward

over the rustling
sheets of leaves.

The End of October

I slide my arms down through and out
the sleeves of an old sweatshirt,
and suddenly my hands emerge

like someone else's, or like something
other than hands—paperbacks,
flexible and worn, easy to carry

one to a pocket. I'll spend all winter
with these two books, anthologies
of my earthly life, collected works

of what I am, dangling there
like growing years or gathered poems,
both full and never complete.

One Leaf

It would fall farther
if it could, pulling
the whole tree with it.

It would fall faster
if possible, marking
time with its sadness.

And it would fall
over and over again,
pulling the world

to its personal autumn.

All Hallows

With the compass
of our oak tree,
the world has drawn
the perfect circle
of a harvest moon.

Having finished its
geometry homework,
the world brushes away
the excess lead
with a hand of breeze.

So much of the world's
other classwork is flawed,
a mess. But for now,
in one small assignment,
here, it is flawless.

Locust Tree

Like a good fire, all evening
this tree has glowed a deep yellow
south of our house, its small leaves
accumulating like embers beneath.

Above it rises the invisible
smoke of loss. Yet another year
flames away up the chimney,
warming the house as it disappears.

Canada Geese

I stepped out back
for more firewood, into
the significant wind
of November. It was cold,
the coldest night so far,
a storm coming in.
Overhead, a small
flock of Canada geese
crossed the moon.

I chose my wood
and scurried back in
while that flock of geese,
bent like an arm,
gathered the best timber
of the dying year:
the moon, the wind,
the storm coming in,
the coldest night so far.

Class

Today before dawn my living room window
is a long chalkboard, beyond which are written,
in the moon's perfect cursive, the lecture notes
of the first hard frost. And all my old teachers,
well-meaning people who have long since passed
out of my life, are here telling me once again
to sit up straight and pay attention.
"Write this down," they say, and point back
at the glittering world. "It's all important."

Weathervane

Wearing my winter coat
for the first time,
I am walking the dog.

In this new cold
I feel as light as wind,
all direction,

breath sharp as an arrow.

Winter Again

And all these dead
sit by their fires,
the hearths and the stoves
of marble or stone.

The trees of their lives
are now the split timber
of dates, of names.
Stoked by this wind,

their logs spark,
and one can hear
the runners creak
on rocking chairs.

They warm themselves
as couples, or alone,
by banked embers
or new glow.

A Marble Earth

—a gift to one of my children

Dark blue, with tiny continents,
including Antarctica and even
an Arctic ice cap, the marble toy
is part of a larger set, the whole
solar system. Yet only this one
appeals to me, like an aerial
photograph of my home, except
here I can roll the picture around
in my hand. Here at long last
I can see the world the way
the great saints, the contemplatives,
the mystics, must have seen it—
small, smooth, marble-hard,
inconsequential, a dark blue toy
given to children. Too often my world
seems atmospheric, topographical,
so big, imperfect, and complicated,
part of no larger system or set,
spinning and orbiting at speeds
unbelievable as I cling to it.
Finally here I have some sense
of otherworldliness, rolling this earth
pole to pole, ocean over continent,
watching it disappear in my hand.

Antaeus

Antaeus the wrestler
perished after Hercules
held him high off
the earth, the source
of his great strength,
strangling him to death.

Just so, this week
we've missed each other
coming and going, Wife.
I've been held high off
the earth of your flesh,
no footing, no breath.

Local Weather

Near-record lows tonight,
the weatherman says, no clouds
in the entire tri-state area.
The ceiling, he says, is unlimited.
This bitter night finds us in bed,
you with a magazine, and I
nodding off through his report,
long day behind, long day ahead.

I click the television off
and curl into you, no clouds
to separate our miniscule home
from the expanse of stars. Under them
you are all I have and need, Wife,
the ceiling over us unlimited.

A Dust of Snow

Like a white cardinal,
it lighted from the branch of a fir,
leaving its perch there.

It flew off
into the white sky of the ground
and disappeared.

Its song,
the white silence of pre-dawn,
split the air.

Custom

Last night, the salt of stars
spilled across the tabletop
of the clear sky. Now at dawn
the sun has thrown a few crystals
over its shoulder, for good luck,
to drive bad spirits away.

Domelight

Overnight, someone left on
this car's interior lamp,
its filament a pulse,
the car itself a shell,
an egg of warmth
at the end of December,
accidental, chick-frail.

Snowplows

An overnight blizzard
has called all these whales
up to the surface again,

and since three a.m.
they've been leaping and crashing
in the new white waves

of our town. Cold metal
reverberates a whale-song
each time one breaks a drift

with its blade, and a flat tail
of gravel slaps the pavement
as it dives again. By dawn

their dalliance will end,
their nimble girth disappear,
their wide wakes remain.

Semi

I walked down Main Street
and the wind was trucking by,
the flat-nosed eighteen-wheeler
of a stiff mid-January breeze.
I tried to read the cab door
and I think it said North Dakota,
but I'm pretty sure the trailer
had Alberta plates. Besides, our town's
one stoplight, flashing yellow,
barely slowed the rig's momentum
as it rolled through, full of diesel
and freighted with a fresh supply
of winter for the coming months.
A long haul lies ahead of it, and us.

Full Moon

This morning's moon, of course, is round,
but somehow it seems a white square,
the first square of a chessboard,

upon which I would love to place
the lone rice-grain of a metaphor,
then double its number each day

for sixty-three more mornings; two,
four, eight, sixteen, and so on
until the number of good poems grows

too large to count by hand, but then
continues to increase by squares,
outnumbering at last the moondust.

Bad Basketball Player

Too short, too slow, no peripheral
vision, no way ambidextrous,
weird shooting form, no vertical:

but most of all because, as guard,
I forced the ball, constantly passed
into traffic, dished off overmuch,

tried way too hard
to make some exotic play happen
when it just wasn't open. Turnover

after turnover, I never learned
in basketball to trust the rhythm,
the motions of a beautiful game

to recommend a pass or play
better than one I could imagine
on my own. I've quit ball

long since, and still I bear
this bad trait. Yet sometimes,
I see now, a gap will open

for the assist, the perfect chance
to feed the beautiful the ball
and let it score. I've learned to wait.

County Snowplow Driver

A blade divides the white waves
south on Highway 15, and a yellow
seaworthy vessel cuts through drifts
like so much foam, its cab a sail
billowed full of coffee steam
and country music. Long before dawn
our explorer rounds Cape Horn
and sails up the Pacific Ocean
of blizzard-packed country roads.
For even a local man can know
the way Magellan must have felt,
being farther out than anyone else
yet can travel, that feeling of being
first and therefore important. Call him
adventuresome or half-crazy
or both, these roads must be opened.
Even around here we need people
willing to circumnavigate the globe
and conquer the unknown, guided
only by stars or by safety lights.

Country Cemetery

A certain magnetism draws you here
to this North Pole,
to its rows of Arctic-white marble and stone.
You've trekked here on the sled of self-pity,
mushing its dogs with a whip.

Here everything arcs away down the globe—
Greenland, Alaska, Siberia
the surrounding fields.
And you are delighted. How quiet, how sun-lit
is the planet's tip.

But once you have stood atop the world
with no one else,
you can go no farther as an explorer.
Longing for home—the whole rest of the earth—
you turn your sled around.

And anywhere you go is south.

DWAINE SPIEKER has been writing for twenty-five
years. After growing up on a farm at the eastern edge of
the Nebraska sandhills, he attended the University of
Nebraska at Kearney and the University of Nebraska-
Lincoln. He now teaches high school English in Wayne,
Nebraska, where he lives with his wife and four children.
His first book of poetry, *Garden of Stars*, won the 2011
Nebraska Book Award for Poetry, and he was recently a
finalist for the 2014 Pablo Neruda Poetry Prize.

Dwaine's books are available on *Amazon.com* and at
www.roguefacultypress.org.

To contact Dwaine, write him at *spiekerfamily@gmail.com*